AN
AVERAGE REVENGE

Sonnets by

JOHN GURNEY

Illustrated by
PAUL PETER PIECH

ACUMEN PUBLICATIONS

1992

Some publications by John Gurney:

The First Frost [verse play] (Interim Press, 1981)
Wheal Zion (Peterloo Poets, 1979)
The Topsail Schooners (Mandeville Press, 1977)
The Failed Mine (Mandeville Press, 1976)

Acknowledgements are due to *Acumen* and *Turret Broadsheets* where some of these sonnets first appeared.

ISBN: 1 - 873161 - 03 - 4   (Pbk)

Published by:

Acumen Publications
6 The Mount
Higher Furzeham
Brixham
South Devon
TQ5 8QY

Printed by:

Starling Press
Newport
Gwent

CONTENTS

WILLIAM

COWPER

COWPER'S MIRROR

I STOOD BY Cowper's mirror. At its back
the mercury was mottled so the room
looked faded, dirty-shadowed, faint grey-black,
a parlour of disaster. In the gloom,
beyond my half-transparent silhouette
were figures in an abstract cloud of mould,
the waistcoat he had died in, small vignettes
of Unwin and of Austen, each as cold
and chill as mid-November. Every shape
each table, bookshelf, bending high-backed chair
was etched there like a sombre astral shade,
an image fixed in limbo, sheer despair.
And voices, too, were starting to abuse.
They whispered of the unamusing Ouse.

CHAUCER AND THE DREAM

C HAUCER knew the meaning of the dream.
    Of course the pulsing rose was never picked:
was not allowed to give a rich red scream
but glowered in the garden, pierced and pricked,
undamaged by *Karezza*.

                                He knew well
that lovely lady waiting in her walls
had really nothing carnal there to sell
but polished every leaf when eyes would fall
upon her, or the soft, effeminate wind
made overtures. All normal games of flame
were disallowed: taboo. The Ideal Mind
alone could use her beauty: free from Shame;
    observing through this dim sublunar murk
    professional virginity at work.

ROCHESTER

WITH ROCHESTER the art of writing songs
went out of English Literature till Blake.
He understood simplicity, the strong
appeal of being brief. Yet he could break
a clear tear from an eye by tenderness
and all-pervasive pathos. Was the last
great seventeenth century lyrist.
                                    Yet excess
destroyed him, and his quick, elastic lust.
His muse was odd. As Edmund Gosse observed,
she loved a wanton tumble in the mud,
a nude illumination. She unnerved
morality and made the goat-heart thud.
   Drunk for years together, finally
   both perished of old age at 33.

TRAHERNE

OF COURSE we put exaggerated stress
on possibility. The will dwells
on the future, and becomes much less
effective as it weaves its various spells
and fantasies. The past, too, plays its part
in spoiling things, its years of shadow-life
where joy was killed.
                        Then there's the present's art
of scattering things, the *theyness* that is rife
in prevalent opinion. The mesh is
complex. Yet I listen still for news
like bright Traherne. Anticipate a bliss
destroying space and time. Where, clear as dew,
in ultimate facticity, his eye
once moved from jewel to jewel and cry to cry.

17, SOUTH MOLTON STREET

THEY'RE AT IT STILL, missing the essential
point, the cosmic view of things, these strollers
down South Molton Street, where London's walls
of yellow stocks are more than metaphors
of separation. Blake knew something of
the truth. I can almost see him now
leaning from that window as he coughs
through workmen's dust. It swirls in sunlight, glows
like universes, sheer unboundedness
an instant, then returns to the familiar,
dead. An architect's decided he will stress
the gap between the keystones and voussoirs
with white paint. It brings the stonework out
like something metaphysical, devout.

SAMUEL TAYLOR COLERIDGE

S.T.C., HIGHGATE

I SUFFER. There's no vision in this place.
Coleridge is lying in the aisle,
quite noseless, with no skin upon his face
his epitaph scarce legible. Its style's
appropriate. The chill of Death in Life
strikes upwards from the grave. The God of Dread
still operates, ubiquitous, is rife.

I tremble, spit a prayer, then hope the dead
can hear it. Feel the stimulus to work.
Yes. That's the way it is. The jet-black beam
still strikes up through the nineteenth century murk.
The Primary Imagination screams
its piercing intuition. Sends this bliss
of inspiration. Then this synthesis.

CONJURING SHELLEY

TONIGHT I TRY to master name and form.
I murmur *moon.* Immediately it seems
a full corn-coloured orb, alert and warm,
is lifting from the fish-dock. Like a dream's,
its light enamels all shapes by the quay,
each mooring where the trawlers fight for space,
transfiguring their scalings.
                                    As the sea
heaves slowly at their cables, now I trace
a new name on the ether. Shelley's. Then
immediately his sailing-boat appears:
he hurtles down the deck as once again
a wave breaks on the beam. His melopoeia
is summoning new thunder, bright blue shafts
of lightning to annihilate his craft.

BYRON, 1824

AT SIX O'CLOCK he got up for a pee
for the last time, and then returned to bed
to curse his doctors. He roared disjointedly.
As leeches bled red streaks across his head
he called out to his troops to follow him
across Lepanto's ramparts, not to fear
death's nothingness. Each pseudonym
was failing. No person could appear
to alter Missolonghi, change the moon
that shone back like a physical decay
from the black lake. Another sudden swoon
removed him from the stage, its rambling play.
    No words were left. No way round the impasse.
    The hero's death was turning to a farce.

EMILY BRONTÏ

EMILY BRONTE

LOVE'S FAR MORE than an expedient
relationship, the simply functional
conjunction of the realist. What's meant
is something more than individual
advantage. There is a different urge
at work. Idealists are well aware
a glorious compulsion comes to merge
like water into water, air in air.
All else is incidental.
                           Brontë too,
though longing for such unity, knew well
love's inundating nature, breaking through
as violent as a bog-burst, like a fell
that tilts upon its side and starts to pour
a wall of mud and boulders, liquid moor.

CLARE AT LIPPETT'S HILL

BUT WHO was there to talk to? Who was there
to listen to his language sparingly
and talk about the badness in the air,
the black melt of the night? And how could trees
communicate, exhausted as they were
by fighting one another and the wind
that tangled up the forest, made a slur
of foliage? Something in the mind
must surely have been longing to confess
to someone non-judgemental, someone who
could listen to his fictions and undress
the wounds of his illusions, find a clue
to understand Clare's fulminating oaths
at women, and their complex underclothes.

MISS ROSSETTI AT CHEYNE WALK

THINGS turned around when Miss Rossetti came.
Her moral melancholia calmed the zoo;
the peacocks ceased their screeching, guilt and shame
inhibited the active kangaroos
that frolicked in the garden. Swinburne's games
were quickly stopped, his limbs no longer flew
stark naked down the bannisters. Things tamed.
Grew seriously self-conscious and subdued.
The red-haired whore felt suddenly absurd;
the models felt uncovered, quickly dressed
like flesh trapped in a flash-house. Sadder than
old rain upon a grave, all hope deferred
her face was cold, aloof. Its eyes expressed
that there was nothing new beneath the sun.

SWINBURNE

SWINBURNE would have loved that sort of day.
I stood for several minutes by his grave
and watched the tide-rip, how the wind would flay
the eager sea. The lime trees pitched and raved
like whipping-women as he lay beneath
a sword, its point a key. The atheist.

I thought of him out crossing Putney Heath,
aged seventy. A failed illuminist.
Just five-feet-four. His body, flogged by blondes,
departing with its strange robotic gait
derided by the boys. Eyes set beyond
the line of the horizon. Never late.
Eager for correction, trousers down
in Wimbledon, inside the *Rose and Crown.*

RECALLING ARNOLD

THE MOON shines like a lighthouse on the straits.
It illustrates the black text of the sea
that moves in with the flood-tide, separates
the north land from the south. Pellucidly
you stand here by the window, watch its flow,
intensify its beauty. At your side
I think of Matthew Arnold, years ago,
just married, how he heard in sighing tides
a Sophoclean sorrow, all the pain
of ruptured love, rebuff, abandonment,
the death of metaphysics. The refrain
continues till you whisper, innocent,
that suffering is sin: this winter night
is brilliant with an undecaying light.

MATTHEW ARNOLD

GERARD MANLEY HOPKINS

HOPKINS BURNS HIS VERSE

HOPKINS burnt his verse. The Jesuit
was winning and his manuscripts of ash
disintegrated gaily. Stanzas split,
flickered like the red residual flash
of a failed love. Each sheet died differently.
Some writhed into the air. Some sighed and rolled
round vowels, or hissed out consonants. He
grinned. So much for metaphor, its old
religious imprecision, its strange
impurity that maimed him like the flame's
bright sadism. He rose. Would rearrange
things differently. Drill life. Shape conscious aims.
  Outside, within the garden, every weed
  stood fuming with its individual creed.

EMILY DICKINSON

SHE LONGED for fusion. In her library
    she read about the Light, as day by day
she planned to lose her ego-boundary
in God, in timeless bliss, transcendence, play
continuing forever the embrace
of one by One. Always dressed in white,
she called for Death. Outside the window, space
seemed less expansive.
                   Each autumnal night
the spider span psychosis, spread the nets
of the Great Weaver. The mushrooms too
stood strange, uncanny, listening in sweat,
besprinkled with the drops of heavy dew.
    Their speech was metaphysical, obscure;
    like all eccentric nature, odd, impure.

EMILY DICKENSON

BEAUDELAIRE

INTERSUBJECTIVITY again
engages my attention as I pass
the north wall of the prison where the rain
streaks *Genevieve's Health Studio.* The glass
is scattered with pink drops. There ash-blond Clare
stands ready with the baby-oil to calm
each itch of synteresis. Beaudelaire
would certainly have loved it, though her charms
are costly. Twelve pounds a simple massage.
Twenty for a full-strip hand-relief.
For thirty he could rub her. She would charge
him sixty for *full sex*—all moral grief
forgotten, as he'd lie there by her side,
his skin soft as an orchid's, purified.

IN THE VALE OF HEALTH

T HE DAY was grey as water. Everywhere
the trees stood with the fixed modality
of architecture. The atmosphere
was stagnant and reflected drearily
from East Heath pond.
                              Apparently we'd come
to Byron St., to stand where Lawrence lived
in 1915. His red-brick home
seemed sombre and expressed no narrative
that quickened our existence. October,
sallow-aired, unhallowed, swam around
the black sash-windows. But no messenger
stepped warmly from the doorway to expound
the grandeur of the sun-self, overthrow
North London with his throbbing after-glow.

TENNYSON'S STATUE

TENNYSON'S no longer what he was
in the old days. The verdigris has gone.
Once he used to stand as bright as grass,
a green illumination. Almost shone!
Lincoln Corporation's seen to that.

Now he's cleanest bronze, scrubbed black, forlorn.
His right hand grips a sombre wide-brimmed hat,
his left palm holds a small plant he has torn
from a wall's hole. How very sad he seems,
perplexed by essences. The inmost thing
eludes him, is demoted to a dream.
The dead metallic flower is suffering
and dying. Yet appearances befool.

Behind him, screams of anguish leave the school.

RUPERT BROOKE, 1911

TOILING ON the honey-seller's lawn,
Brooke wrestled with the term *hamartia*.
That blameless sin, that intellectual flaw
evaded clear translation. Grantchester
was flourishing, midsummered, as he marked
that error is our nature, what we see
is tainted almost wholly by the dark
deceptions of our blindness. Tragedy
was gathering as Nemesis prepared
his *seelenbruchenliede*. Many nights
he'd run down to the Cam, strip naked, bare
the foulness of his limbs and, full of spite,
gesticulated wildly, floating by
and fingering derision at the sky.

WILFRED OWEN

CAPTAIN OWEN

IT COMES AGAIN, that old long-focus view
across the Allied Front. There, in the
middle distance, just recently renewed
a line of wire entanglement. To right, a
bomb-catcher. In front, a multitude
of corpses, though the nature of the ground
conceals them. War-land. The view is crude
yet subtle. Occasionally the sounds
of hate return, the khaki-coloured plan
in which one shape is Owen, almost sane:
the self-appointed spokesman for the man
he's killing. His hand shakes once again
as once more his machine-gun company
rakes nothing, stirs the salient, aimlessly.

YEATS, 1938

YEATS DECAYS. He mutters to himself.
He feels the chill of death, thinks fitfully.
Plato and Plotinus line his shelf.
His modern myths no longer signify.
Nothing's quite the way that he supposed.
His clothes unweave with strange textorial fears.
A dangerous hiatus must be closed
between the worlds of sense and of ideas.
His garden sprawls with grasses, fallen weeds.
Leaves tumble like the lower gods that die.
Persephone inspects no more the seeds,
controls things with her supervising eye.
The swan looks sad, and dips her yellow neb.
The spider leaves a torn, unfinished web.

AUDEN

RETICULATED, woven like a net,
Auden's skin is far from luminous.
Screwed up by a million cigarettes
his eyes look lonely, rather dangerous.
The flesh is split. But nothing can be done.
No miracle can change it, no white lead
rejuvenate its texture, no slick pun
relax it back to flatness. It looks dead.
No foreign protein now can penetrate
that epidermis, no cream moisturize
its mask of human suffering, that strange hate
that lingers in his features, nor disguise
how Age, the boy-eternal's enemy,
has little to reveal but irony.

PHILIP LARKIN

LARKIN

SUDDENLY I've found why I am here
  out walking Fish Dock Three, upon its quay,
at Grimsby. The lock-pit now appears.
Is open to the inflow of the sea
at the wall's end. Its concrete, low and squat
is finished by a siren. Now a gull
wails.
      There comes the thought of Larkin in that
last year, dying, suffering in Hull,
editing his minutes, fingering books
on the still shelves. I stiffen, smell his dread.
Ships grunt up the Humber. Something's hooked
in the far depths. It lifts up from its bed
its cry of lamentation, now incites
this echo-note of mourning through the night.

DATTA, DAYADHVAM, DAMYATA

REVEALING and concealing who you are,
you whisper thunder. Is it Eliot
who speaks, or some inspired familiar?
I listen, till I feel an idiot,
tormented. Initially I'm sure
all substance seemed implosive, everywhere.
Silence was a menace to endure
in terror, though in time the filthy air
turned spirit. It was then the reeking earth
firmed, no longer slipped like liquid. Things
were churned towards a process of rebirth
by whirlpool. And the gap round everything
was altered, uncontaminated, clear,
illuminated, now, and always here.